EMMANUEL JOSEPH

Sonic Oratory, Weaving Music and Sound into the Fabric of Your Speeches

Copyright © 2025 by Emmanuel Joseph

All rights reserved. No part of this publication may be reproduced, stored or transmitted in any form or by any means, electronic, mechanical, photocopying, recording, scanning, or otherwise without written permission from the publisher. It is illegal to copy this book, post it to a website, or distribute it by any other means without permission.

First edition

This book was professionally typeset on Reedsy. Find out more at reedsy.com

Contents

1	Chapter 1: The Symphony of Speech	1
2	Chapter 2: The Rhythm of Rhetoric	3
3	Chapter 3: The Melody of Meaning	5
4	Chapter 4: The Harmony of Connection	7
5	Chapter 5: The Dynamics of Delivery	9
6	Chapter 6: The Tempo of Timing	11
7	Chapter 7: The Resonance of Repetition	13
8	Chapter 8: The Cadence of Clarity	15
9	Chapter 9: The Echo of Emotion	17
10	Chapter 10: The Harmony of Humor	19
11	Chapter 11: The Silence of Significance	21
12	Chapter 12: The Crescendo of Conclusion	23
13	Epilogue: The Legacy of Sonic Oratory	25

1

Chapter 1: The Symphony of Speech

Every speech is a performance, a delicate dance between words and emotions. Just as a composer arranges notes to create harmony, a speaker must orchestrate their words to resonate with their audience. The rhythm of your voice, the pauses between sentences, and the cadence of your delivery are the instruments of your sonic oratory. When you begin to think of your speech as a musical composition, you unlock the potential to move people not just intellectually, but emotionally. The power of sound lies in its ability to bypass logic and touch the soul, creating a connection that words alone cannot achieve.

Music has long been a universal language, transcending barriers of culture, age, and experience. By infusing your speeches with musical elements, you tap into this ancient form of communication. Consider how a crescendo can build anticipation, or how a sudden silence can command attention. These techniques are not just tools for musicians; they are tools for speakers who wish to captivate their audience. The key is to understand the emotional weight of sound and use it to amplify your message.

To master sonic oratory, you must first become a listener. Pay attention to the sounds around you—the rise and fall of a conversation, the rhythm of footsteps, the melody of laughter. These everyday sounds are your teachers, showing you how to craft a speech that feels alive. When you listen deeply, you begin to hear the music in language, the subtle harmonies that make a

SONIC ORATORY, WEAVING MUSIC AND SOUND INTO THE FABRIC OF YOUR SPEECHES

speech unforgettable. This awareness is the foundation of sonic oratory.

As you embark on this journey, remember that your voice is your instrument. It has its own unique timbre, pitch, and range. Just as a musician practices scales, you must practice your delivery, experimenting with tone, volume, and pace. Over time, you will discover the sounds that resonate most powerfully with your audience. This is the art of sonic oratory: weaving music and sound into the fabric of your speeches, creating a tapestry of words and emotions that lingers long after the final note.

2

Chapter 2: The Rhythm of Rhetoric

Rhythm is the heartbeat of speech, the pulse that gives it life. Just as a song relies on its beat to drive the melody forward, a speech relies on its rhythm to engage the audience. A well-paced speech is like a well-composed piece of music: it flows naturally, carrying the listener along with it. To master the rhythm of rhetoric, you must learn to balance speed and slowness, knowing when to quicken the tempo and when to slow it down.

One of the most powerful tools in your arsenal is the pause. A pause is not an absence of sound; it is a presence of anticipation. It gives your audience time to absorb your words, to reflect on their meaning, and to prepare for what comes next. A well-timed pause can be as impactful as a thunderous crescendo, creating a moment of tension that draws the audience in. Use pauses strategically, allowing them to punctuate your speech like rests in a musical score.

Another key element of rhythm is repetition. Just as a chorus repeats in a song, certain phrases or ideas can be repeated in a speech to reinforce their importance. Repetition creates a sense of familiarity, making your message more memorable. However, like any musical technique, it must be used sparingly. Too much repetition can become monotonous, losing its impact. The goal is to create a rhythm that feels natural and compelling, guiding your audience through your speech with ease.

SONIC ORATORY, WEAVING MUSIC AND SOUND INTO THE FABRIC OF YOUR SPEECHES

Finally, consider the rhythm of your sentences. Short, staccato sentences can create a sense of urgency or excitement, while longer, flowing sentences can evoke calm or contemplation. By varying the length and structure of your sentences, you create a dynamic rhythm that keeps your audience engaged. This is the essence of the rhythm of rhetoric: using the musicality of language to craft a speech that resonates with the heart as well as the mind.

3

Chapter 3: The Melody of Meaning

Every word you speak carries a melody, a tonal quality that conveys emotion and intent. The melody of meaning is the emotional undercurrent of your speech, the subtle shifts in tone that give your words depth and resonance. Just as a musician uses melody to express feelings, a speaker uses tone to connect with their audience on an emotional level. To master the melody of meaning, you must become attuned to the emotional nuances of your voice.

One way to enhance the melody of your speech is through inflection. Inflection is the rise and fall of your voice as you speak, the subtle variations in pitch that add color to your words. A monotone voice can make even the most exciting topic seem dull, while a voice rich in inflection can bring even the simplest words to life. Experiment with different inflections, noticing how they change the emotional tone of your speech. A rising inflection can convey curiosity or excitement, while a falling inflection can suggest certainty or finality.

Another important aspect of melody is emphasis. By stressing certain words or phrases, you highlight their importance and guide your audience's attention. Think of emphasis as the accents in a musical piece, the moments that stand out and grab the listener's ear. When you emphasize a word, you give it weight, making it more memorable. Use emphasis to underscore key points, to convey passion, or to create contrast.

The melody of meaning also involves the emotional tone of your speech. Just as a song can be joyful, somber, or triumphant, your speech can convey a range of emotions through your tone. Consider the emotional journey you want your audience to take, and adjust your tone accordingly. A warm, inviting tone can create a sense of connection, while a serious, solemn tone can convey gravity and importance. By mastering the melody of meaning, you transform your speech into a symphony of emotions, leaving a lasting impression on your audience.

4

Chapter 4: The Harmony of Connection

Harmony is the blending of different elements to create a unified whole. In music, harmony is the combination of notes that complement each other, creating a richer, more complex sound. In speech, harmony is the connection between you and your audience, the alignment of your message with their emotions and values. To achieve harmony in your speeches, you must understand your audience and tailor your message to resonate with them.

One way to create harmony is through empathy. Empathy is the ability to understand and share the feelings of others, to see the world through their eyes. When you speak with empathy, you create a sense of connection, showing your audience that you understand their hopes, fears, and desires. This connection is the foundation of harmony, the bridge that links your words to their hearts. To cultivate empathy, listen to your audience, observe their reactions, and adjust your message accordingly.

Another key to harmony is authenticity. Just as a dissonant note can disrupt a musical piece, a lack of authenticity can undermine your speech. Your audience can sense when you are being genuine and when you are not. To create harmony, you must speak from the heart, sharing your true thoughts and feelings. Authenticity builds trust, making your audience more receptive to your message. When you are authentic, your words carry a sincerity that resonates deeply.

Harmony also involves balance. Just as a musical piece balances different instruments and melodies, a speech must balance different elements: logic and emotion, structure and spontaneity, simplicity and complexity. Too much of one element can throw off the balance, making your speech feel lopsided or disjointed. Strive for a harmonious blend of these elements, creating a speech that is both engaging and coherent.

Finally, harmony is about unity. Just as a choir blends individual voices into a single, harmonious sound, a speech unites the speaker and the audience in a shared experience. When you achieve harmony, your speech becomes more than just words; it becomes a moment of connection, a shared journey of discovery and inspiration. This is the power of sonic oratory: to weave music and sound into the fabric of your speeches, creating a harmony that lingers long after the final word.

5

Chapter 5: The Dynamics of Delivery

Dynamics in music refer to the variations in volume and intensity, the shifts between loud and soft, powerful and delicate. In speech, dynamics are equally important, adding depth and texture to your delivery. A monotone voice can quickly bore an audience, while a dynamic delivery keeps them engaged and attentive. To master the dynamics of delivery, you must learn to modulate your voice, using volume and intensity to emphasize key points and create emotional impact.

One way to enhance your dynamics is through vocal projection. Projection is the ability to make your voice heard clearly and confidently, even in a large space. A strong, projected voice commands attention, while a weak, muffled voice can be easily ignored. Practice projecting your voice, ensuring that every word reaches your audience with clarity and power. However, be mindful of balance; too much volume can overwhelm, while too little can be inaudible.

Another aspect of dynamics is intensity. Intensity is the emotional energy behind your words, the passion and conviction that make your message compelling. When you speak with intensity, your audience feels your commitment and is more likely to be moved by your words. Intensity can be conveyed through your tone, your gestures, and your facial expressions. Use intensity to highlight key moments in your speech, creating peaks of emotion that captivate your audience.

SONIC ORATORY, WEAVING MUSIC AND SOUND INTO THE FABRIC OF YOUR SPEECHES

Dynamics also involve contrast. Just as a musical piece alternates between loud and soft passages, a speech should vary in intensity and volume. Contrast creates interest, keeping your audience engaged and curious about what comes next. For example, you might begin a sentence softly, drawing your audience in, and then crescendo to a powerful conclusion. This contrast adds drama and impact to your delivery, making your speech more memorable.

Finally, dynamics are about control. Just as a musician must control their instrument to produce the desired sound, a speaker must control their voice to achieve the desired effect. Practice modulating your voice, experimenting with different levels of volume and intensity. Over time, you will develop the ability to use dynamics instinctively, enhancing your delivery and creating a more engaging and impactful speech.

6

Chapter 6: The Tempo of Timing

Tempo in music refers to the speed at which a piece is played, from the slow, languid pace of a ballad to the fast, energetic beat of a dance track. In speech, tempo is equally important, influencing the mood and impact of your words. A well-timed speech is like a well-timed piece of music: it flows smoothly, keeping the audience engaged and attentive. To master the tempo of timing, you must learn to control the pace of your delivery, knowing when to speed up and when to slow down.

One way to control tempo is through pacing. Pacing is the rhythm of your speech, the speed at which you deliver your words. A fast pace can create excitement and urgency, while a slow pace can convey calm and reflection. However, it's important to vary your pacing, as a constant speed can become monotonous. Use faster pacing to build momentum and slower pacing to emphasize key points, creating a dynamic and engaging rhythm.

Another aspect of tempo is timing. Timing is the art of knowing when to speak and when to pause, when to rush and when to linger. A well-timed pause can create suspense, while a poorly timed one can disrupt the flow of your speech. Practice your timing, paying attention to the natural rhythm of your words and the reactions of your audience. Over time, you will develop a sense of timing that enhances your delivery and keeps your audience engaged.

Tempo also involves adaptability. Just as a musician adjusts their tempo to suit the mood of a piece, a speaker must adjust their pace to suit the context of their speech. For example, a formal presentation may require a slower, more measured pace, while a motivational speech may benefit from a faster, more energetic tempo. Be mindful of the setting and the audience, and adjust your tempo accordingly.

Finally, tempo is about flow. Just as a musical piece flows from one note to the next, a speech should flow seamlessly from one idea to the next. Avoid abrupt transitions or sudden changes in pace, as these can disrupt the flow and confuse your audience. Instead, aim for a smooth, natural progression, guiding your audience through your speech with ease. This is the essence of the tempo of timing: using the speed and rhythm of your delivery to create a speech that is both engaging and impactful.

7

Chapter 7: The Resonance of Repetition

Repetition is a powerful tool in both music and speech, creating a sense of familiarity and reinforcing key ideas. In music, a repeating melody or chorus can make a song more memorable. In speech, repetition can make your message more impactful, driving home your points and leaving a lasting impression. To master the resonance of repetition, you must learn to use it strategically, knowing when and how to repeat your words for maximum effect.

One way to use repetition is through the rule of three. The rule of three is a rhetorical technique that involves repeating a word or phrase three times for emphasis. This technique is effective because it creates a rhythm that is easy to remember and reinforces the importance of the repeated idea. For example, you might say, "We must work hard, we must work together, and we must work with passion." The repetition of "we must work" drives home the message, making it more memorable.

Another aspect of repetition is the use of refrains. A refrain is a phrase or sentence that is repeated at regular intervals throughout a speech, much like a chorus in a song. A well-chosen refrain can create a sense of unity and coherence, tying your speech together and reinforcing your central theme. For example, you might use the refrain "Together, we can achieve greatness" at key moments in your speech, creating a rallying cry that inspires your audience.

Repetition also involves variation. Just as a musical piece might repeat a melody with slight variations, a speech can repeat an idea with different phrasing or emphasis. This keeps the repetition from becoming monotonous, adding interest and depth to your message. For example, you might repeat the idea of "perseverance" in different ways, such as "We must never give up," "We must keep pushing forward," and "We must persist against all odds." This variation keeps the message fresh while reinforcing its importance.

Finally, repetition is about impact. Just as a repeating drumbeat can create a sense of urgency, a repeated phrase can create a sense of urgency or importance in your speech. Use repetition to highlight key points, to create a sense of rhythm, and to leave a lasting impression on your audience. This is the power of the resonance of repetition: using the echo of your words to amplify your message and make it unforgettable.

8

Chapter 8: The Cadence of Clarity

Cadence in music refers to the sequence of chords that brings a piece to a satisfying conclusion. In speech, cadence is the rhythm and flow of your words, the way they rise and fall to create a sense of closure. A well-crafted cadence can make your speech more memorable, leaving your audience with a clear and lasting impression. To master the cadence of clarity, you must learn to structure your speech in a way that builds to a powerful conclusion.

One way to create cadence is through sentence structure. Just as a musical phrase has a beginning, middle, and end, a sentence should have a clear structure that guides the listener to a satisfying conclusion. Use shorter sentences to create a sense of urgency and longer sentences to build anticipation. Vary your sentence length to create a natural rhythm, leading your audience through your speech with ease.

Another aspect of cadence is the use of climax. A climax is the high point of your speech, the moment of greatest intensity and impact. Just as a musical piece builds to a crescendo, your speech should build to a climax, drawing your audience in and leaving them breathless. Use your climax to deliver your most important point, the idea you want your audience to remember long after your speech is over.

Cadence also involves resolution. Just as a musical piece resolves to a final chord, your speech should resolve to a clear and satisfying conclusion. This resolution provides closure, tying together the threads of your speech and leaving your audience with a sense of completeness. Use your conclusion to summarize your key points, to inspire your audience, or to call them to action. A well-crafted conclusion is the final note in your cadence, the moment that leaves your audience with a lasting impression.

Finally, cadence is about flow. Just as a musical piece flows from one note to the next, your speech should flow seamlessly from one idea to the next. Avoid abrupt transitions or sudden changes in tone, as these can disrupt the flow and confuse your audience. Instead, aim for a smooth, natural progression, guiding your audience through your speech with ease. This is the essence of the cadence of clarity: using the rhythm and flow of your words to create a speech that is both engaging and impactful.

9

Chapter 9: The Echo of Emotion

Emotion is the heart of any speech, the force that connects you to your audience and makes your message resonate. Just as a musician uses melody and harmony to evoke feelings, a speaker uses words and tone to stir emotions. To master the echo of emotion, you must learn to tap into the emotional undercurrents of your speech, using them to create a powerful and lasting impact.

One way to evoke emotion is through storytelling. Stories have the power to transport your audience, to make them feel as if they are experiencing the events you describe. When you tell a story, you create an emotional connection, drawing your audience into your world and making your message more relatable. Use vivid imagery, sensory details, and emotional language to bring your stories to life, creating a tapestry of words that resonates with your audience.

Another aspect of emotion is tone. Your tone is the emotional quality of your voice, the way it conveys your feelings and intentions. A warm, inviting tone can create a sense of connection, while a serious, solemn tone can convey gravity and importance. Use your tone to match the emotional content of your speech, ensuring that your words and your voice are in harmony. When your tone aligns with your message, your audience is more likely to feel the emotions you wish to convey.

Emotion also involves vulnerability. Just as a musician bares their soul through their music, a speaker must be willing to share their true feelings with their audience. Vulnerability creates authenticity, showing your audience that you are human and relatable. When you speak from the heart, your words carry a sincerity that resonates deeply. Don't be afraid to show your emotions, whether it's joy, sadness, or passion. Your vulnerability will create a powerful echo, touching the hearts of your audience.

Finally, emotion is about connection. Just as a musical piece connects the musician and the listener, a speech connects the speaker and the audience. When you evoke emotion, you create a shared experience, a moment of connection that transcends words. This connection is the essence of the echo of emotion: using the power of feeling to create a speech that resonates deeply and leaves a lasting impression.

10

Chapter 10: The Harmony of Humor

Humor is a powerful tool in speech, capable of breaking down barriers, building rapport, and making your message more memorable. Just as a musician uses a playful melody to lighten the mood, a speaker can use humor to engage their audience and create a sense of connection. To master the harmony of humor, you must learn to use it wisely, knowing when and how to inject levity into your speech.

One way to use humor is through anecdotes. A well-told anecdote can make your audience laugh while also illustrating a key point. When choosing an anecdote, look for stories that are relatable and relevant to your message. Avoid jokes that are offensive or overly complex, as these can alienate your audience. Instead, opt for lighthearted, self-deprecating humor that shows your human side and makes your audience feel at ease.

Another aspect of humor is timing. Just as a comedian relies on timing to deliver a punchline, a speaker must use timing to maximize the impact of their humor. A well-timed joke can break the ice, lighten the mood, or emphasize a point. However, poorly timed humor can fall flat or disrupt the flow of your speech. Practice your timing, paying attention to the natural rhythm of your words and the reactions of your audience. Over time, you will develop a sense of timing that enhances your humor and keeps your audience engaged.

Humor also involves balance. Just as a musical piece balances different elements, a speech must balance humor with seriousness. Too much humor can undermine your message, making your speech feel frivolous or insincere. Too little humor can make your speech feel dry or overly formal. Strive for a harmonious blend of humor and seriousness, using humor to enhance your message without overshadowing it.

Finally, humor is about connection. Just as a shared laugh can bring people together, humor can create a sense of camaraderie between you and your audience. When you make your audience laugh, you create a moment of connection, a shared experience that transcends words. This connection is the essence of the harmony of humor: using the power of laughter to create a speech that is both engaging and impactful.

11

Chapter 11: The Silence of Significance

Silence is one of the most powerful tools in a speaker's arsenal, capable of creating suspense, emphasizing a point, and giving your audience time to reflect. Just as a musician uses rests to create tension and release, a speaker can use silence to enhance the impact of their words. To master the silence of significance, you must learn to embrace the power of the pause, using it strategically to create a more dynamic and impactful speech.

One way to use silence is through anticipation. A well-timed pause can create a sense of anticipation, drawing your audience in and making them eager to hear what comes next. Use pauses before delivering a key point or a punchline, allowing the silence to build tension and heighten the impact of your words. This technique is particularly effective in storytelling, where a pause can create a moment of suspense that keeps your audience on the edge of their seats.

Another aspect of silence is reflection. A pause can give your audience time to absorb your words, to reflect on their meaning, and to prepare for what comes next. Use pauses after delivering a key point, allowing your audience to process the information and internalize its significance. This reflective silence creates a moment of connection, showing your audience that you value their understanding and engagement.

Silence also involves control. Just as a musician must control their instrument to produce the desired sound, a speaker must control their delivery to use silence effectively. Avoid filling pauses with filler words like "um" or "uh," as these can undermine the impact of the silence. Instead, embrace the pause, allowing it to stand on its own as a powerful tool in your speech. Practice your delivery, experimenting with different lengths and placements of pauses. Over time, you will develop the ability to use silence instinctively, enhancing your speech and creating a more engaging and impactful experience for your audience.

Finally, silence is about significance. Just as a rest in a musical piece can create a moment of profound beauty, a pause in a speech can create a moment of profound impact. Use silence to emphasize key points, to create a sense of drama, and to give your audience time to reflect. This is the essence of the silence of significance: using the power of the pause to create a speech that resonates deeply and leaves a lasting impression.

12

Chapter 12: The Crescendo of Conclusion

Every speech is a journey, a progression from the opening notes to the final crescendo. The conclusion is the climax of your speech, the moment when all the elements come together to create a powerful and lasting impact. To master the crescendo of conclusion, you must learn to build to a satisfying finale, leaving your audience with a clear and memorable impression.

One way to create a crescendo is through summation. A well-crafted conclusion summarizes your key points, tying together the threads of your speech and reinforcing your central message. Use your conclusion to remind your audience of the journey you've taken together, highlighting the most important ideas and insights. This summation creates a sense of closure, leaving your audience with a clear understanding of your message.

Another aspect of the crescendo is inspiration. A powerful conclusion can inspire your audience, leaving them with a sense of hope, motivation, or determination. Use your conclusion to call your audience to action, to challenge them to think differently, or to encourage them to pursue their goals. An inspirational conclusion creates a lasting impact, motivating your audience to take your message to heart and apply it in their own lives.

The crescendo also involves emotion. Just as a musical piece builds to an emotional climax, your conclusion should evoke a strong emotional response. Use your tone, your words, and your delivery to create a moment of emotional intensity, leaving your audience moved and inspired. Whether it's joy, sadness, or passion, the emotional resonance of your conclusion will linger long after your speech is over.

Finally, the crescendo is about impact. Just as a musical piece ends with a final, powerful chord, your speech should end with a final, powerful statement. This statement is your last chance to leave a lasting impression, so make it count. Use a memorable phrase, a striking image, or a compelling call to action to create a conclusion that resonates deeply with your audience. This is the essence of the crescendo of conclusion: using the power of your final words to create a speech that is both impactful and unforgettable.

13

Epilogue: The Legacy of Sonic Oratory

Sonic oratory is more than just a technique; it is an art form, a way of weaving music and sound into the fabric of your speeches to create a lasting impact. When you master the elements of sonic oratory—rhythm, melody, harmony, dynamics, tempo, repetition, cadence, emotion, humor, silence, and crescendo—you transform your speeches into symphonies of words and sound, captivating your audience and leaving them inspired.

The legacy of sonic oratory is the legacy of connection. When you speak with the power of music and sound, you create a moment of connection, a shared experience that transcends words. This connection is the heart of great oratory, the force that moves people to action, to change, to greatness. As you continue to refine your craft, remember that your voice is your instrument, and your speeches are your compositions. Use them wisely, and let the music of your words echo in the hearts of your audience, creating a legacy that endures long after the final note

Book Description: "Sonic Oratory: Weaving Music and Sound into the Fabric of Your Speeches"

Imagine a speech that doesn't just inform or persuade, but *moves* people—deeply, emotionally, and memorably. A speech that feels less like a presentation and more like a symphony, where every word, pause, and tone is carefully orchestrated to resonate with the audience. This is the essence of

SONIC ORATORY, WEAVING MUSIC AND SOUND INTO THE FABRIC OF YOUR SPEECHES

Sonic Oratory, a groundbreaking exploration of how to weave the principles of music and sound into the art of public speaking.

In this book, you'll discover how to transform your speeches into powerful, immersive experiences by tapping into the universal language of sound. Drawing on the parallels between music and speech, you'll learn how to use rhythm to captivate, melody to evoke emotion, and harmony to connect with your audience on a profound level. From the subtle power of silence to the dynamic impact of crescendos, each chapter unveils practical techniques to elevate your speaking craft.

Whether you're a seasoned speaker or just starting out, *Sonic Oratory* offers a fresh perspective on how to engage, inspire, and leave a lasting impression. Through relatable examples, actionable insights, and a touch of creativity, this book will help you unlock the musicality of your voice and the artistry of your words. By the end, you'll not only deliver speeches—you'll create moments of magic that linger in the hearts and minds of your audience long after you've left the stage.

This is more than a book about public speaking; it's a guide to becoming a maestro of communication, where every speech is a performance and every word is a note in a larger, unforgettable composition. Let *Sonic Oratory* be your guide to crafting speeches that don't just speak—they sing.

www.ingramcontent.com/pod-product-compliance
Lightning Source LLC
LaVergne TN
LVHW010444070526
838199LV00066B/6192